Meats & Poultry

HEALTHFUL KOREAN COOKING

by Noh Chin-hwa
Copyreader: Shirley A. Dorow

HOLLYM

First published in 1985
Sixth printing, 1994
by Hollym International Corp.
18 Donald Place
Elizabeth, New Jersey 07208 U.S.A.
Phone: (908) 353-1655   Fax: (908) 353-0255

Published simultaneously in Korea
by Hollym Corporation; Publishers
14-5 Kwanchol-dong, Chongno-gu,
Seoul 110-111, Korea
Phone: (02) 735-7554   Fax: (02) 730-5149

ISBN : 0-930878-46-9
Library of Congress Catalog Card Number: 85-80450

Printed in Korea

CONTENTS

About the Author

The author, Noh Chin-hwa, graduated from Seoul National University with a degree in Home Economics. Since her marriage she has put her natural talent in cooking as well as in flower arranging and painting to good use.

Applying her creative power to cooking she has contributed articles and pictures to women's magazines, and she used to give lectures at Home Economics' College and Women's Institutes. She also has introduced Korean cuisine, Chinese cooking and Western cooking through television, radio and magazines and has published several books including the Traditional Korean Cooking Series and Daily Card Menus.

Currently she leads an active life as head of the Munhwa Cooking School and representative director of the Korea Flower Arrangement Society.

Author: Noh Chin-hwa

About the Copyreader

The English-language copyreader for this cookbook, Shirley A. Dorow, has lived in Seoul, Korea since 1958 with her husband, Maynard W. Dorow, who is a missionary with the Lutheran church. They have four grown children.

During her more than 25 years in Korea Mrs. Dorow's hobby has been cooking with foods from the Korean markets. She has a collection of Korean food slides and has presented several Food Forum slide-talks for newcomers about western-style cooking using Korean market foods. She also wrote a food column for the Korea Times.

Mrs. Dorow is a graduate of Valparaiso University, Valparaiso, Indiana with a B.A. in sociology and religion and has licensure in early childhood education. She taught at Seoul Foreign School for 9½ years.

Copyreader: Shirley A. Dorow

4

INTRODUCTION

This cookbook of Korean recipes in English has been prepared for the English reader with the hope that westerner cooks might experience truly authentic Korean dishes. Until now many Korean cookbooks have been presented in English, but they present only those recipes which westerners are presumed to prefer and they modify the recipes for western taste.

This cookbook is authentically Korean. It is a careful translation of recipes prepared by a woman who directs a Korean cooking school in Seoul, Korea for real Korean housewives who are actually using these recipes daily. Even the Korean style layout of the book is the same style as in Korean cookbooks and magazine cooking columns today.

It is true that these recipes stem from age-old Korean traditional recipes and as such are scintillating combinations of food and seasoning unique to the Korean heritage. It is also true, however, that Korean cooking is known for its individual touches. Each family has its own way of seasoning, and brides new to a certain family live with the mother-in-law, even today, long enough to learn these subtle nuances in cooking for their husbands.

The western reader, too, may wish to vary the ingredients according to individual taste. This is acceptable Korean-style cooking. However the recipes presented here present the current vogue based on years of refinement by the collective Korean palate.

Some of these recipes are presented in English for the first time. The step-by-step photo sequences make preparation quite easy and the glossary will help readers understand each individual ingredient and thereby develop a feel for the total impact intended in each recipe.

This book is presented in the hope that gourmet cooks interested in Oriental cookery may extend their repertoire of truly good food and enjoy authentic Korean cooking.

Seoul, Korea

Shirley A. Darow

PREPARATION TIPS

Korean food preparation methods are quite different from western ones. The main jobs in preparing a Korean meal are the cutting, slicing, seasoning and careful arranging of the food.

The cutting of foods before cooking is very important for appearance as well as convenience in eating with chopsticks. Slicing, chopping, scoring and sectioning the vegetables, fish and meat are techniques employed so that the food will cook quickly and be easier to eat. Also, each ingredient is cut or sliced into the same size or shape and the same thickness so that it cooks evenly and looks neat. Because of the quick cooking the nutritional value remains high as well. Scoring, which is the process of cutting slits in the meat, allows the marinade to penetrate further into meats and also prevents the cooked meat from curling up during cooking. Chopping the seasonings (such as garlic, green onion and ginger) allows for better distribution of the flavor throughout the dish.

Various seasoning sauces are used for marinating meat or fish before broiling or stir-frying. Other sauces are used on vegetables. The amounts of seasonings used may vary with one's preference and other ingredients may also be added to suit one's individual taste.

Some of the sauces are these:

1. Seasoning soy sauce: Combine 4 tbsp. soy sauce, 2 tbsp. sugar, 1 tbsp. rice wine, 1 tbsp. chopped green onion, 1 tbsp. chopped garlic, 1 tbsp. sesame oil, 1 tbsp. sesame salt (crushed sesame that has been toasted with a little salt added), and black pepper to taste. Pine nuts and extra rice wine are optional.

2. Sweet sauce: Combine 1 cup soy sauce, ½ lb. dark corn syrup, ⅓ cup sugar, ⅔ cup water, 1 tbsp. ginger juice or flat slices of fresh ginger, ¼ cup rice wine, 1 tsp. black pepper, and a little MSG in a pan and simmer on low heat until thick.

3. Vinegar-soy sauce: Combine 4 tbsp. soy sauce, 1 tsp. sugar, ½ tbsp. sesame salt, 2 tsp. vinegar, chopped green onion and garlic to taste.

4. Mustard-vinegar sauce: Slowly stir ½ cup boiling water into 7 tbsp. mustard powder; stir until a smooth paste forms in the bowl. Put the bowl containing the mustard paste upside down on a hot cooking pot (perhaps one where rice is cooking) and let it stand for 10-15 minutes. When the mustard is somewhat translucent add 1 tbsp. soy sauce, 3 tbsp. sugar, ½ cup vinegar and 1 tsp. salt and mix well.

5. Seasoned red pepper paste: Combine 2 tbsp. red pepper paste, 2 tbsp. soy sauce, 1 tbsp. chopped garlic, 2 tbsp. chopped green onion, 1 tbsp. sugar, 1 tbsp. sesame salt, and 2 tbsp. sesame oil in a pan and simmer on low heat until thick.

The final step in preparing most dishes is the careful arranging of the foods paying particular attention to alternating the natural colors of the foods to make a pleasant pattern. Foods are always arranged neatly in concentric circles, radial designs or parallel linear columns and never placed in a disorderly fashion. The dish must have eye appeal when presented for eating and recipes often give directions for the exact arrangement of the foods. The photos illustrate this important part of Korean cookery clearly as well.

The recipes in this book will generally serve 4-6 persons.

In the recipes in this book quantities are given in American standard cup and spoon measurements and metric measure for weight.

THE KOREAN DIET

For centuries the Koreans have eaten the fruits of the sea, the field and the mountain because these are the geographically significant features of the Korean peninsula.

The Yellow Sea and Sea of Japan offer excellent fish, seaweed and shellfish for the Korean table. The lowland fields produce excellent grains and vegetables while the uplands grow marvelous fruits and nuts—apple, pear, plum, chestnut, walnut, pine nut and persimmon to name a few. And the ever-present mountains offer wild and cultivated mushrooms, roots and greens. A temperate climate makes for four seasons with the fall harvest being the most abundant. Through the centuries the basic seasonings—red pepper, green onion, soy sauce, bean pastes, garlic, ginger, sesame, mustard, vinegar and wines—have been combined various ways to enhance the meats, fish, seafood and vegetables in the peculiarly spicy and delicious Korean manner. Various regions of Korea have special seasoning combinations—some hotter, some spicier—and each family also has its particular seasoning pattern. One family uses no salted shrimp juice in kimchi; another uses a great deal, but both claim kimchi as an integral part of their daily diet.

Kimchi is a kind of a spicy fermented pickle and accompanies every Korean meal. It is made from cabbage, turnip, cucumber or seasonable vegetables, seasoned with red pepper, garlic, onion, ginger, salt, oysters and soused salted fish juice, and fermented in an earthenware crock. Kimchi is made in large quantities in late autumn for use during the winter months. Autumn kimchi making is called kimjang which is one of Korea's most important household events. Kimchi contains good amounts of vitamin C and stimulates the appetite. Somehow, kimchi and rice make an excellent flavor and texture combination.

The basic diet includes at each meal steamed rice, hot soup, kimchis and a number of meat and/or vegetable side dishes with fruit as an after-meal refresher. In-season fresh vegetables are used at the peak of their season and dried or preserved for out-of-season use later on.

Korean table settings are classified into the 3-chop, the 5-chop, the 7-chop, the 9-chop and the 12-chop setting according to the number of side dishes served. The average family takes three or four side dishes along with rice, soup and kimchi for an everyday Korean meal.

When a family entertains guests for a special occasion, such as a wedding celebration or 60th birthday party, a dozen or more delightful dishes of different kinds are served according to the season. In addition, there is a characteristic way of setting the table for each occasion: New Year's Day Table, Moon-Festival Day Table, Baby's First Birthday Table, Ancestor-Memorial Day Table, Bride's Gift Table or Drinking Table.

Korean food is usually shared by diners. Each person has his own bowl of rice and soup, but other dishes are set on the table for all to reach. The main dishes and the side dishes are distinguished by the quantities served. At meal time, the smaller quantity of the food served will be one of the side dishes. Larger quantity dishes will be the main dish and nothing more will be needed except rice and kimchi.

As for the serving, all the food dishes except hot soups are set at one time on a low table that is set on the floor; at which one sits to eat. The main dishes and the side dishes which are shared by all are placed in the middle of the table. The rice and soup are placed in front of each diner. Chopsticks and spoons are used for eating.

In general the Korean diet is high in grains and vegetables which add much fiber to the diet, moderate but adequate in protein, both animal and vegetable (bean curd, bean sprouts, bean pastes, soy bean sauce), moderate in calories and low in fat and sugar. In short—a very healthy, well-balanced diet. It may be a bit high in salt if soy sauce is used heavily. It may or may not be red peppery hot; it is a matter of individual taste.

The Korean diet is changing and developing but basically the diet pattern has remained the same. Westerners may do well to examine this diet pattern and shift to a similar diet pattern for their own long and healthy life.

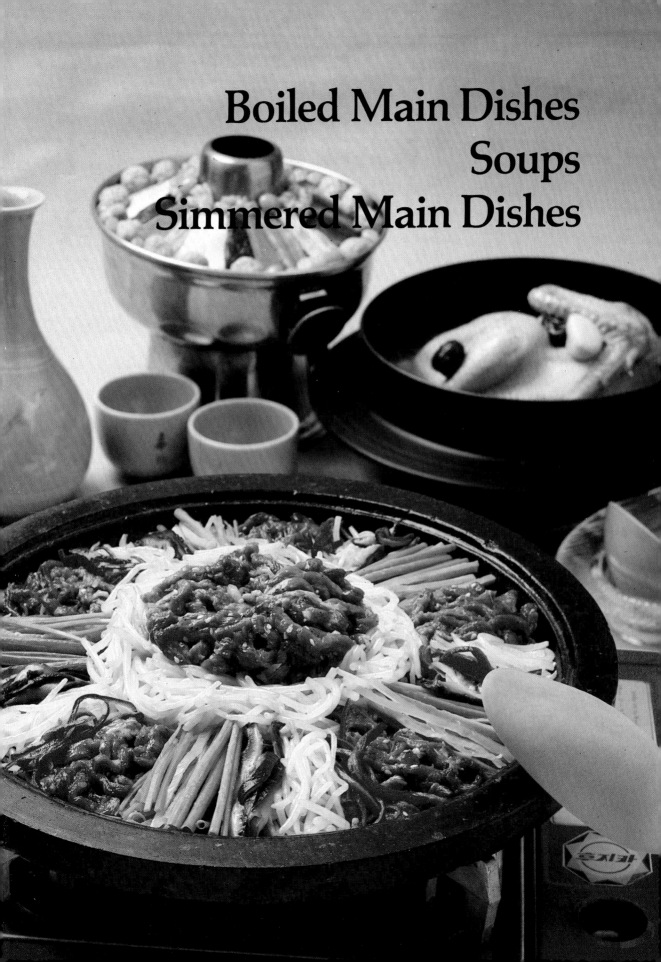

Boiled Main Dishes
Soups
Simmered Main Dishes

Beef Stock Soup
Komt'ang (곰탕)

Ingredients 1⅓ lb. shank of beef, ½ whole Korean white radish, ¼ lb. Chinese noodles, 1 large green onion, 5 cloves garlic, salt, black pepper, MSG

Method 1 Cut the beef into large pieces and halve the radish. Boil the beef and radish in 30 cups of water. Lower the heat and simmer for 1 hour until the meat is very tender.

2 Take the meat and radish out of the broth. Cool the broth and skim off excess fat that has floated to the top. Slice the meat thinly into bite-sized pieces cutting against the grain. Slice the radish into pieces ⅛″ thick.

3 Add the meat, radish and crushed garlic to the broth. Then bring to a boil again.

4 Cut large green onion into rings. Add the salt, black pepper and green onion and check the seasoning just before serving.

Hint This beef stock soup may be made using the knuckle bone.

. Cut the meat into large pieces.

2 Halve the whole radish.

3 Remove the meat and radish from the broth when cooked.

4 Strain the broth to remove excess fat.

5 Slice thinly cutting against the grain.

6 Boil the meat and radish in the broth.

Beef Rib Soup
Kalbit'ang (갈비탕)

Ingredients   1⅓ lb. beef, ⅓ Korean white radish, green onion, garlic, 1 egg, 1 tbsp. soy sauce, salt, black pepper, MSG, 15 cups broth

Method   **1** Cut the ribs into pieces 1⅔" long and score them at ⅓" intervals. Halve the white radish lengthwise.
2 Fry the beaten, salted yolk and white of egg separately into sheets and cut into thin strips. Chop the green onion and garlic finely.
3 Boil the ribs and radish with 30 cups of water in a large pot. Remove the radish from the broth when cooked and simmer the ribs for about 2 hours until very tender.
4 Take the ribs out of the broth and slice the radish thinly. Then mix the ribs and radish with the soy sauce, black pepper, sesame oil, green onion and garlic.
5 Cool the broth and skim off excess fat from the top.
6 Put the seasoned ribs and radish into the broth and bring to a boil again. Season with black pepper and MSG.
7 Check the seasoning and place the beef rib soup in each bowl. Garnish with egg strips.

Hint   **1** Scoring the ribs cross-grain makes them easier to eat.
2 The soup may be saltier when cooled, so add salt sparingly when seasoning.

1 Score the ribs.

2 Fry the beaten yolk and white of egg separately into thin sheets.

3 Season the ribs and radish.

4 Boil the seasoned ribs and radish in the broth.

Beef Rib Soup

Spicy Beef Soup
Yukkaejang (육개장)

Ingredients   ½ lb. beef, ½ lb. tripe, ½ lb. small beef intestine, ⅓ lb. fern bracken, 4 large green onions, black pepper, MSG, seasoning sauce: (3 tbsp. red pepper paste, 9 cloves garlic, 5 tbsp. sesame salt, sesame oil, 4 tbsp. red pepper powder, 4 tbsp. salad oil), 15 cups broth

Method   **1** Wash the beef.

2 Wash and soak the tripe in hot water. Then scrape off the black skin with the back of a knife.

3 Remove any fat from the small intestine and cut it into pieces. Wash the pieces clean scrubbing with coarse salt.

4 Simmer the beef, tripe and small intestine in 30 cups of water for 2 hours until very tender.

5 Shred the beef into thick strips. Cut the tripe into pieces 2¾″ long and ¼″ wide. Cut the small intestine into bite-sized pieces.

6 Clean the bracken and green onions and cut them into 4¾″ lengths.

7 Put the above ingredients (except the green onions) in a bowl and mix them with the seasoning sauce.

8 Mix and fry the oil and red pepper powder in a pan to make the red pepper oil.

9 Add the **#7** seasoned ingredients and 15 cups of the broth to the pan and bring to a boil. Add the green onion slices and boil slightly again.

Spicy Beef Soup

1 Remove any fat from the beef intestine.

2 Mix the bracken, onion, meat and small intestine with the seasoning.

3 Make the red pepper oil.

4 Add the broth and **#2** to **#3** and bring to a boil.

13

Meatball Soup
Wanjakuk (완자국)

1 Finely mince the beef.

3 Sieve the mashed bean curd.

5 Shape the mixture into meatballs 1″ in diameter.

2 Wrap the bean curd in a cloth and squeeze it tightly.

Ingredients ¼ lb. ground beef, garland chrysanthemum, ½ square onion, 1 egg, ½ tsp. salt, ½ tsp. soy sauce, ½ tsp. sesame oil, ½ tsp. sesame salt, 2 tbsp. flour, 7 cups broth

Method **1** Chop the beef and garlic finely.
2 Wrap the bean curd in a clean cloth and squeeze out the excess water. Sieve the mashed bean curd.

4 Mix the meat and bean curd with the seasoning.

3 Mix #1 and #2 with the soy sauce, salt and sesame salt.
4 Shape the #3 mixture into meatballs 1″ in diameter. Dip each meatball into flour.
5 Pour the broth into a pan and season it with soy sauce and salt.

6 Add the meatballs dipped into beaten egg to the boiling broth.

When the broth boils, add the meatballs dipped into beaten egg and bring to a boil again. Float the garland chrysanthemum leaves on the top and serve.
Hint **1** Use finely ground or minced beef so that the meatballs will not break.
2 Oil both hands to form well-rounded meatballs.

14

Spring Chicken Soup
Yŏnggyebaeksuk (영계백숙)

Ingredients 1 spring chicken, ½ cup glutinous rice, 10 cloves garlic, 6 jujubes, 6 chestnuts, 1 knob ginger, salt, black pepper, MSG

Method 1 Remove the organs, lower legs, feet and head from the chicken and clean.

2 Stuff the chicken cavity with the glutinous rice and 5 cloves of garlic. Sew the body cavity shut.

3 Put the stuffed chicken in a pot and add water enough to simmer. Add the jujubes, peeled chestnuts, ginger and remaining cloves of garlic. Cover the pot and bring to a boil. Then reduce the heat and simmer for 1 hour.

4 Add the salt, black pepper and sliced green onion just before eating.

Hint 1 Stuff the chicken cavity with only a little glutinous rice, leaving room for it to expand as it cooks.

2 For medicinal use, take the boiled chicken out of the broth, add ginseng root and simmer the broth again.

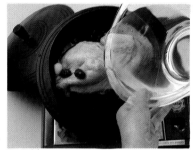

1 Stuff the chicken cavity with the glutinous rice and garlic.

2 Sew the body cavity shut.

3 Add water enough to simmer.

Fancy Hot Pot
Shinsŏllo (신선로)

Ingredients **A** ⅓ lb. ground beef, 3 tbsp. cornstarch powder, 1 egg, various seasonings
B ¼ lb. beef liver, ¼ lb. white fish fillets, ½ tsp. salt, ½ tsp. black pepper, flour, 1 egg
C 2 eggs, 2 oz. carrot, 3 dried brown, oak mushrooms, ½ bundle watercress, flour, 30 gingko nuts, 5 walnuts, 5 stone mushrooms
D 2 oz. beef strips, ½ round onion, 1 dried brown, oak mushroom

Method **1** Mix the ground beef, cornstarch powder and egg with various seasonings reserving one-third of the mixture for meatballs.

2 Heat a well-oiled square fry pan. Spread the #1 mixture on the hot pan and fry it until well-done. Then cut the fried meat mixture into bite-sized pieces. Use the reserved one-third of the meat mixture to form meatballs ⅓" in diameter. Dip each ball in flour and beaten egg and brown in oil.

3 Slice the liver flatly and soak it in cold water to remove the blood. Season the liver slices with the **B** ingredients and dip them into flour, then into beaten egg and brown in oil.

4 Slice the fish into bite-sized pieces and mix it with the **B** seasonings. Dip each piece into flour and then

5 Add the fried liver slices.

6 Garnish the top with the gingko nuts, walnuts and meatballs.

16

into beaten egg and brown in oil.

5 Slice 2 oz. beef, ½ round onion and 1 dried mushroom into thin strips and mix them with the seasonings. Layer them in the bottom of the shinsollo pot.

6 Make a second layer with the fried liver, fish and meat slices.

7 Cut the carrot into the same lengths as the radius of the shinsollo pot and ½" wide.

8 After soaking the dried mushrooms in water, squeeze out the excess water. Cut them into the same size as the carrot rectangles.

9 Remove the leaves from the watercress and skewer the stems together evenly.

10 Soak the shelled walnuts in hot water, drain and peel off the dark skin.

11 Fry the shelled ginko nuts slightly in a greased pan and remove the skins chafing them with a clean paper.

12 Dip the **#9** skewered watercress into flour and then into beaten egg and brown in oil.

13 Fry the beaten egg yolk and white separately into thin sheets. Cut the egg sheets into the same size as the carrot rectangles.

14 Arrange the prepared vegetable and egg rectangles attractively alternating colors in a spoke fashion on top of the other layers. Garnish with the gingko nuts, walnuts and meatballs.

15 Add meat broth to the shinsollo and heat, or add water to the shinsollo and bring it to a quick boil; serve and eat. (The shinsollo pan may be heated with charcoal or canned heat in its center core.)

1 Mix the ground beef, cornstarch powder and egg with the seasonings.

2 Fry the meat mixture in a square fry pan.

3 Cut the fried meat mixture into bite-sized pieces.

4 Place a layer of the seasoned beef, onion and mushrooms in the bottom.

Method for Vegetable-Beef Simmered Dish

1 Mix the sliced beef with the seasonings.

2 Remove the seeds from the peppers and slice them into thin strips.

3 Mix the sliced onion, dried mushrooms and beef with the seasonings.

4 Arrange all the sliced ingredients alternating colors.

5 Place the mung-bean sprouts and beef in the center.

6 Pour the hot meat-broth over the top.

Ingredients 1 lb. beef, 7 dried brown, oak mushrooms, ¼ carrot, ⅓ lb. mung-bean sprouts, 2 oz. small green onion, 3 red peppers, 1 round onion, 1 tbsp. sugar, 1 tbsp. rice wine, 3 tbsp. soy sauce, 1 tbsp. sesame salt, 2 tbsp. chopped green onion, 2 tsp. garlic, black pepper, salt, MSG

Method 1 Cut the beef into thin strips, mix with the seasonings and let it stand. Slice the round onion into thin strips.

2 Soak the dried mushrooms in

Vegetable-Beef Simmered Dish
Soegogi Chön-gol (쇠고기 전골)

water and remove the stems. Slice thinly and fry them lightly with the sesame oil, soy sauce and sugar.

3 Remove the beans and hairlike tips from the mung-bean sprouts and scald them slightly. Drain and mix them with the salt and sesame oil.

4 Cut the carrots into thin strips 2″ long. Cut the small green onion into the same lengths.

5 Halve the red peppers, remove the seeds and cut the peppers into thin strips.

6 Place the sliced round onion, ¹/₆ dried mushroom and ¹/₆ beef in the center of the pot.

7 Pile the beef and bean sprouts in the center of the pan and colorfully arrange the carrot, small green onion, mung-bean sprouts, dried mushrooms, red peppers and beef around them.

8 Make meat broth and season it with the salt, black pepper and MSG. Add the meat broth to #7 and boil briefly at the table.

Hint. By marinating the beef in the sugar and rice wine first, the meat will be tender and will not give off an odor. Mung-bean sprouts do not remain tasty if rinsed in cold water.

Method for Beef Intestine Simmered Dish

1 Rub the intestine with salt to clean.

2 Soak the tripe in hot water to remove the black skin.

3 Remove the thick cabbage stems.

4 Season the tripe and intestine.

18

Beef Intestine Simmered Dish
Kopch'ang Chŏn-gol (곱창 전골)

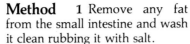

Ingredients　**A** 1 lb. beef small intestine, ½ lb. tripe, ½ lb. shank of beef, 2 large green onions
B 5 dried brown, oak mushrooms, ⅓ carrot, ¼ lb. cabbage, 2 round onions, ¼ lb. thick noodles, 4 cups broth, ½ oz. garland chrysanthemum
C 3 tbsp. red pepper paste, 2 tbsp. soy sauce, 2 tsp. sugar, 6 tbsp. green onion, 3 cloves garlic, 2 tbsp. sesame salt, 2 tsp. sesame oil, 2 tbsp. red pepper powder; final seasonings: (2 tbsp. soy sauce, 1 tsp. green onion, 1 clove garlic, 4 tbsp. anchovy broth, 2 tsp. sesame salt, black pepper)

Method　**1** Remove any fat from the small intestine and wash it clean rubbing it with salt.
2 Soak the tripe in hot water and drain. Remove the black skin by scraping with a spoon and wash it clean.
3 Wash the shank of beef and cut it into bite-sized pieces.
4 Put the **#1, #2, #3** ingredients with 30 cups of water in a large pot. Bring to a boil on high heat and then simmer for 1 hour on medium heat until tender.
5 Take the meat out of the **#4** liquid and cut it into bite-sized pieces. Mix well with the **C** ingre-

dients and place it in a heavy, flat chongol pot.
6 Soak the dried mushrooms in water and remove the stems. Cut X slits on them.
7 Halve the carrot and cut it diagonally into crescent-shaped pieces.
8 Remove the stems from the cabbage and cut the leaves into ¾"×1¼" pieces.
9 Cut the round onions into the same size as the carrot pieces.
10 Cook the thick noodles in boiling water and rinse them in cold water. Drain.
11 Arrange the **#6, #7, #8, #9** vegetables in the **#5** pot attractively. Pour 4 cups of the **#4** broth over the vegetables and bring to a boil. When the vegetables are tender, place the noodles in the center and sprinkle them with the final seasonings. Add garland chrysanthemum leaves on the top.

5 Cut the onion.

6 Arrange the ingredients in a shallow cooking pan.

Simmered Chicken Dish
Takkogi Chŏn-gol (닭고기 전골)

1 Remove the meat from the bones.

2 Fry the shelled ginko nuts with salt.

3 Place the hot ginko nuts on paper and rub off the skins.

4 Shape the sliced jellied potato-cake like maejagwa.

5 Season the chicken and dried mushrooms separately.

6 Place the chicken in the center of a shallow cooking pan.

Ingredients   ⅔ lb. chicken, 5 dried brown, oak mushrooms, ⅓ carrot, 2 oz. small green onions, 1 round onion, 2 oz. watercress, 2 oz. garland chrysanthemum, ⅓ lb. konyak: jellied potato-cake (used like a noodle), 20 gingko nuts, 2 eggs, 1 green onion, 4 cloves garlic, ginger juice, 2 tbsp. soy sauce, 1 tbsp. sesame oil, 1 tbsp. sesame salt, 1 tbsp. red pepper powder, 1½ tbsp. sugar, 1 tbsp. red pepper paste, salt, black pepper, MSG

Method   1 Prepare the legs and breast of the chicken by removing the meat from the bones and cutting it into thin strips. Simmer the bones to make the chicken broth.

2 Soak the dried mushrooms in water, remove the stems and cut them into thin strips. Cut the round onion and carrot into thin strips.

3 Cut the small green onions and watercress into 2″ lengths.

4 Peel and fry the gingko nuts in an oiled pan. Place them on paper and rub off the top-skins.

5 Cut the konyak into ⅛″ thick and ¾″ × 2¾″ pieces. Slit each piece down the center leaving the ends intact and twist one end through the slit to shape it like maejagwa, thin Korean cookies.

6 Mix the green onion, chopped garlic, soy sauce, black pepper, sesame oil and salt to make the seasoning sauce. Season the chicken and dried mushroom strips separately.

7 Place the seasoned chicken in the center of a shallow cooking pan, surrounded by the prepared vegetables. Pour the broth over the ingredients and bring to a boil. When the flavor has developed, add the ginko nuts and garland chrysanthemum and bring to a boil and serve.

Hint   The konyak is absorbed in this chicken dish making it more flavorful.

Stews
Stir-Fried Dishes
Soy-Sauce-Glazed Dishes

Beef Rib Stew
Soegalbitchim (쇠갈비찜)

Ingredients   4 lb. beef ribs, 4½ tbsp. sugar, 3 tbsp. rice wine, ½ cup chopped green onion, 1 tbsp. garlic, 9 tbsp. soy sauce, 2 tbsp. sesame salt, 2 tbsp. sesame oil, black pepper, MSG, 2 carrots, 15 chestnuts, 20 gingko nuts, 10 jujubes, 1 Korean white radish, 2 round onions, 3 cups water, 3 tbsp. pine nuts

Method   **1** Have the butcher cut the ribs into pieces 2⅓" long. Wash and score them diagonally at ⅓" intervals. Marinate them in the sugar and rice wine for 10 minutes.

2 Mix the garlic, green onions, soy sauce, sesame salt, sesame oil, black pepper and MSG to make the seasoning sauce.

3 Cut the carrots and white radish into chestnut-sized pieces.

4 Peel the chestnuts and clean the jujubes.

5 Peel and fry the shelled ginko nuts in an oiled pan until they turn green. Rub off the top-skins.

6 Fry the **#3, #4** and **#5** ingredients lightly in an oiled pan.

7 Cut the remaining carrot and round onions into thin strips.

8 Place the **#7** ingredients in the bottom of a pan and make a second layer with the ribs dipped into the seasoning sauce, leaving the center empty. Add 3 cups of water and cover. Boil hard for 20 minutes and then simmer for 30 minutes on medium heat. Add the prepared gingko nuts and simmer for 10 minutes more.

9 When the ribs and other ingredients become tender, remove the lid and simmer them on high heat until glazed.

10. Arrange the **#9** food attractively on a plate and sprinkle with the finely chopped pine nuts.

Hint   **1** Though you cook a large quantity of ribs, 3 cups of water should be sufficient.

2 When the gingko nuts are cooked, add the broth and simmer on high heat.

1 Score the ribs diagonally at ⅓" intervals.

2 Marinate the ribs in the sugar and rice wine.

3 Cut the radish and carrots into chestnut-sized pieces.

4 Place the ribs dipped into the seasoning sauce on top of the onion.

5 Top the ribs with the garnish.

6 Simmer the ingredients on high heat until glazed.

Beef and Vegetable Stew
Soegogi Yach'aetchim (쇠고기 야채찜)

Ingredients   **A** 1 lb. beef, 5 large cabbage leaves
B ½ cup cornstarch powder, ½ egg, 6 tbsp. chopped green onion, 2 tbsp. garlic, 1 tbsp. rice wine, 2 tbsp. soy sauce, ½ tbsp. sesame oil, 1 tbsp. sugar, 1 tbsp. sesame salt, 1 tsp. salt, black pepper, MSG
C ½ carrot, 2 green peppers, 2 oz. mung-bean sprouts, parsley, cherries

Method   **1** Remove the vein stems from the cabbage leaves and cut the leaves into 4" square pieces. Scald in salted boiling water and rinse them in cold water. **2** Cut the carrot into ¼" thick pieces and scald and cut them into ¼" cubes. Halve the green peppers to remove the seeds and cut them into ¼" square pieces. Scald the mung-bean sprouts, squeeze and chop them finely.

3 Mix the minced beef and sliced vegetables well with the **B** ingredients. Shape the mixture into oval meatballs in the palm of your hand and dip them in starch powder.
4 Dip the insides of the cabbage leaves in cornstarch powder. Place each meatball in the cabbage leaf and wrap it into a small bundle.
5 Place the cabbage bundles in a steamer and steam for 15 minutes.

1 Remove the vein stems from the cabbage leaves.

2 Scald and cut the vegetables finely.

3 Stuff the meatballs into the leaves making small bundles.

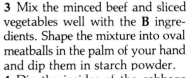

4 Steam the cabbage bundles for 15 minutes.

Pork Rib Stew
Twaejigalbitchim (돼지갈비찜)

Ingredients **A** 1⅓ lb. pork ribs, 2 tbsp. salad oil
B 2½ tbsp. soy sauce, 1½ tbsp. sugar, 6 tbsp. green onion, 2 tbsp. garlic, 2 tbsp. ginger juice, 2 tbsp. rice wine
C pine nuts, ⅓ carrot, 20 gingko nuts, 2 potatoes, 2 green peppers, 2 jujubes

Method **1** Have the butcher cut the spareribs into 2″ long pieces and score them on both sides.
2 Stir-fry the ginko nuts in a lightly salted pan until they turn green color. Then rub off the top-skins.
3 Fry the spareribs in a heated oiled pan until brown.

Remove excess oil and place the ribs in another pan.
4 Add half of the mixed **B** ingredients and 2 cups water to the **#3** ribs and simmer them on high heat for 10 minutes.
5 When the ribs are tender, add the gingko nuts, the carrots and potatoes cut into flower shapes and the remaining seasoning and stir-fry until glazed.
6 Place the seasoned ribs and vegetables in a serving dish and garnish with the sliced jujube and powdered pine nuts.

2 Fry the ribs in a heated oiled pan until brown.

4 Add half of the **B** seasonings to **#3** and simmer.

1 Score the spareribs at ⅓″ intervals.

3 Place the ribs in another pan.

5 Add the remaining seasoning and stir, frying lightly.

Steamed Pork with Vegetables
Twaejigogi Saektchim (돼지고기 색찜)

Ingredients ⅔ lb. pork, ⅓ cucumber, ¼ carrot, 1 dried brown, oak mushroom, 2 stone mushrooms, egg sheets, salt, black pepper, 3 tbsp. sated shrimp juice, 1 tsp. ginger juice, MSG, pine nuts

Method 1 Cut the pork (leaving on the fat) into pieces 3″×2″. Bind it tightly with a cotton thread and boil. Remove the fat from the boiled pork and trim it into a piece ⅛″ thick. Cut slits in the pork

and place on top of the piece of fat.
2 Cut the cucumber and carrot into thin strips and fry lightly. Fry the yolk and white of egg separately into sheets and cut them into thin strips.
3 Cut the dried mushroom and stone mushrooms into thin strips.
4 Place the above ingredients in the slits of the #1 boiled pork alternating colors. Sprinkle the top evenly with salted shrimp juice and ginger juice and steam for 5 minutes.

1 Tie the pork with the cotton thread.

2 Cut slits in the boiled pork.

3 Cut the carrot into thin strips and fry.

4 Stuff the slits with the vegetables alternating colors.

5 Sprinkle the top with salted shrimp juice and ginger juice and steam.

27

Noodles with Beef and Vegetables
Soegogi Chapch'ae (쇠고기 잡채)

Ingredients **A** ⅓ lb. beef, 2 tbsp. soy sauce, 1 tbsp. sugar, 1 tbsp. green onion, 1 clove garlic, black pepper, 1 tbsp. sesame oil
B ⅓ lb. Chinese noodles (tangmyon), 1½ tbsp. soy sauce, 1 tbsp. sugar, 1 tbsp. sesame salt
C ⅓ carrot, 2 oz. bellflower roots, 1 clove garlic, ½ tsp. salt, 1 round onion, 5 dried brown, oak mushrooms, soy sauce, sugar, sesame oil, ½ bun- dle watercress, 1 tsp. salt
D 1 egg, 1 stone mushroom, pine nuts
Method **1** Using tender beef, cut it into thin strips and let it stand in the **A** seasoning sauce.
2 Cut the carrot into thin strips and fry it lightly adding salt in an oiled pan.
3 Scald the bellflower roots in boiling water and shred them finely. Fry them lightly adding chopped

1 Cut the beef into thin strips and marinate in the seasoning.

4 Scald the bellflower roots in boiling water.

5 Scald Chinese noodles, drain and mix with sesame oil.

2 Cut the carrot into 2" lengths.

6 Stir-fry the beef and then the dried mushrooms.

3 Stir-fry the carrot with salt.

7 Stir-fry all the ingredients lightly and season to taste.

28

garlic and salt.

4 Halve and cut the round onion into thin strips and fry adding salt.

5 Cut the watercress into 2″ lengths and fry lightly adding salt.

6 Cook Chinese noodles in boiling water until soft and rinse in cold water. Cut them into 8″ lengths and mix with sesame oil.

7 Fry the marinated beef with the dried mushrooms and sprinkle with sugar and soy sauce.

8 Stir-fry the **#6** noodles seasoning to taste with soy sauce, sugar and sesame salt. Combine all the pre-pared ingredients thoroughly and season with the sesame oil, black pepper and MSG.

9 Place the **#8** mixture on a plate and garnish with the egg yolk strips, stone mushroom strips and pine nuts.

Hint **1** When stir-frying each ingredient, begin with the light-colored ones. Fry the beef and dried mushroom last.

2 Add the watercress later so as to keep the fresh green color.

Stir-Fry Beef with Peppers
Soegogi P'utkoch'ubokkŭm (쇠고기 풋고추볶음)

Ingredients ½ lb. beef tenderloin, 1 tbsp. rice wine, 2 tsp. soy sauce, ½ tsp. salt, 1 tsp. sugar, 1 tbsp. cornstarch powder, 3 oz. Korean green pepper, 3 red peppers, 3 cloves garlic, 1 tbsp. oil, 1 tsp. salt, ½ tsp. sugar

Method 1 Cut the beef into thin strips and season it with the rice wine, sugar, soy sauce, salt, and cornstarch powder. Let it stand for 10 minutes.
2 Cut the green peppers into thin strips and soak them in water to remove the "hot" taste.
3 Slice the garlic into flat pieces.
4 Stir-fry the green pepper and red pepper strips lightly with the salt and sugar in an oiled pan.
5 Stir-fry the garlic and seasoned beef in a lightly oiled pan. Add the **#4** peppers and stir-fry again.

Hint Fry the green peppers only slightly to keep the color clear. Green peppers contain much vitamin A.

1 Wash the sliced peppers and drain.

2 Fry the pepper lightly with the salt and sugar.

3 Fry the garlic, beef and add the **#2** pepper mixture last of all.

30

Stir-Fry Rice Cake
Ttŏkpokkŭm (떡볶음)

Ingredients **A** ⅔ lb. rice cake
B ¼ lb. beef, 1 tbsp. soy sauce,
½ tbsp. sugar, 1 tbsp. green onion,
1 clove garlic, 1 tsp. sesame salt,
½ tbsp. sesame oil
C ¼ lb. carrot, 2 oz. bamboo
shoots, 3 dried mushrooms, ½ cucumber, ½ cup water
D 1 tsp. soy sauce, ½ tbsp. sugar
Method **1** Cut the sticks of
rice cake into 1⅔″ lengths and
divide them into lengthwise quar-

ters. Scald in boiling water and
rinse in cold water.
2 Cut the beef into thick strips
and season it with the **B** ingredients. Cut the carrots, bamboo
shoots, dried mushrooms and
cucumber into 1⅔″ long, flat rectangles.
3 Fry the seasoned beef in a pan
until cooked and add the vegetables, rice cake and water and
bring to a boil. Season with the **D**

sugar and soy sauce and stir well.

1 Cut the sticks of rice cake into 1⅔″
lengths and scald and rinse them in
cold water.

2 Fry the green onion, garlic and beef
and add the water.

3 Add the rice cake and vegetables to
#2 and cook briefly. Add the cucumber later and fry again lightly.

31

Stir-Fry Pork
Twaejigogibokkŭm (돼지고기볶음)

Ingredients   ⅔ lb. pork, 1 round onion, 2 Korean green peppers, 2 Korean red peppers, 3 tbsp. oil, ¼ cup water, seasoning sauce: (2 tbsp. soy sauce, 1 tbsp. green onion, 1 tsp. garlic, 2 tbsp. red pepper paste, 1 knob ginger)

Method   **1** Chop the ginger finely.
2 Cut the pork into 1⅔" thick, flat pieces and mix it with the seasoning sauce.
3 Halve the green peppers, remove the seeds and cut them into piece ⅓" × ½". Cut the round onion into the same-sized pieces.
4 Fry the marinated pork in a heated oiled pan, add the above vegetables and stir-fry lightly.

Stir-Fry Pork with Vegetables

Stir-Fry Pork

Stir-Fry Pork with Vegetables
Twaejigogi Yach'aebokkŭm (돼지고기 야채볶음)

Ingredients ⅓ lb. pork, 3 tbsp. cornstarch powder, ¼ lb. carrot, 1 can of bamboo shoots, 3 dried brown, oak mushrooms, 1 round onion, ½ cucumber, 10 quail eggs, 2 tbsp. soy sauce, 1 tsp. green onion, 1 clove garlic, 1 tsp. ginger juice, salt, ½ tsp. sesame oil, 1 cup broth, 2 tbsp. cornstarch liquid

Method **1** Slice the pork thinly into pieces 2"×¾". Sprinkle it with salt, black pepper and 3 tbsp. cornstarch powder.
2 Halve the carrot lengthwise and cut it diagonally into piece ¹/₁₀" thick.
3 Cut the bamboo shoots and cucumber diagonally into crescent shapes.
4 Soften the dried mushrooms in water and remove the stems. Slice them into pieces ⅓" wide.
5 Cut the round onion into thick strips.

6 Heat the oil in a pan. Then stir-fry the carrot, dried mushrooms, bamboo shoots, round onion and boiled quail eggs lightly adding them in order. Place them on a plate.
7 Re-oil the pan and stir-fry the garlic until savory. Then add the **#1** pork and fry lightly.
8 Mix the **#7** pork and the **#6** ingredients. Season it with salt, soy sauce, sugar and ginger juice and fry again.
9 Pour the seasoned broth on this mixture and bring to a boil. Thicken the broth by pouring in 2 tbsp. starch liquid. Add the cucumber and sesame oil last of all.

Hint **1** Add the cucumber later to keep the color green. It changes to a yellow color if added first.
2 Add the sesame oil last to retain its special flavor and smell.

Method for Stir-Fry Pork with Vegetables

1 Sprinkle the bite-sized pieces of pork with the salt, black pepper and starch powder.

2 Stir-fry the carrot, dried mushroom, bamboo shoot, round onion and quail eggs in order.

3 Stir-fry the seasoned meat.

4 Mix **#2**, **#3** well and season with salt and soy sauce.

5 Add the starch liquid and broth to **#4**.

Method for Stir-Fry Pork

1 Cut the pork into 1⅔" thick pieces and mix it with the seasoning sauce.

2 Cut the peppers and round onion into square pieces.

3 Stir-fry the marinated pork adding ½ cup water.

4 When almost cooked, add the **#2** vegetables and fry lightly.

33

Stir-Fry Pork with Kimchi
Twaejigogi Kimch'ibokkŭm (돼지고기 김치볶음)

Ingredients **A** ⅔ lb. pork (with fat and skin remaining), ⅔ lb. kimchi, 2 Korean green peppers, 1 red pepper, ½ round onion
B 3 tbsp. red pepper paste, 1 tbsp. chopped green onion, 1 tsp. sugar, sesame salt, black pepper, sesame oil, ½ tbsp. chopped garlic

Method **1** Cut the pork into flat pieces.
2 Combine the **B** ingredients to make the seasoned red pepper paste.
3 Add the **#2** seasoned paste to the pork, mix well and allow it to stand for a while.
4 Remove the stuffing from the kimchi squeezing out the water. Slice it into flat pieces.
5 Halve the green peppers to remove the seeds and cut them into thick strips.
6 Cut the round onion into thin strips.
7 Fry the pork lightly first and then add the **#4, #5, #6** ingredients and stir-fry once again.

Hint This food is delicious served with hot bean curd cut into small pieces.

1 Cut the pork into flat pieces.

2 Combine the **B** ingredients to make the seasoned red pepper paste.

3 Cut the green peppers into thin strips and the kimchi into flat pieces.

4 Fry the seasoned pork and then the sliced vegetables.

Broiled Chicken Giblets
Tangnaejangbokkŭm (닭내장볶음)

Ingredients ⅔ lb. chicken gizzards and livers, 3 dried brown, oak mushrooms, ¼ lb. bamboo shoots, ⅓ lb. konyak: jellied potato-cake, 2 green bell peppers, 4 cloves garlic, 2 tbsp. salad oil, 2 tbsp. soy sauce, salt, ginger juice, black pepper, MSG, 2 tsp. cornstarch powder, ⅓ cup meat broth, 1 tbsp. rice wine, 1 tomato

Method **1** Peel off the inner skin from the chicken gizzards and clean them by scrubbing with salt. Slit the outer part of the gizzards. Then cut them with the chicken livers into bite-sized pieces.

2 Scald the gizzards and livers and rinse in cold water.

3 Soften the dried mushrooms in water, remove the stems and slice them thinly. Cut the bamboo shoots into flat pieces.

4 Slice the jellied potato-cake into 2¾″ × ¾″ × ¼″ thick pieces. Slit each piece down the center leaving the ends intact and twist one end through the slit.

5 Halve the green bell peppers, remove the seeds and cut them into thick strips.

6 Fry the chicken giblets with the chopped garlic and ginger juice in a heated oiled pan. Then add the dried mushroom, jellied potato-cake and bamboo shoot, fry lightly and season them with the soy sauce, sugar, salt and black pepper.

7 Dissolve the cornstarch powder in ⅓ cup broth. Add this starch liquid to the **#6** fried ingredients and bring to a boil to thicken.

1 Slit the outer part of the chicken gizzards.

3 Add the vegetables and fry lightly.

2 Scald the gizzards and livers in boiling water.

4 Add the starch liquid and boil until thick.

Spring Chicken Stew
Yonggyebokkŭm (영계볶음)

Ingredients   1¾ lb. whole spring chicken, ⅓ cup tiny soused, salted shrimp, 5 tbsp. chopped green onion, 1 tbsp. chopped garlic, 1 tbsp. ginger juice, 1 tbsp. sesame oil, 2 tbsp. sesame salt, black pepper, 5 red peppers, 5 green peppers, 1 round onion

Method   1 Cut the chicken into 1⅔" pieces, mix with the salted shrimp and seasoning and let stand.

2 Fry the seasoned chicken lightly in a pan. Pour in enough water to cover the chicken and simmer on low but steady heat.

3 Cut the round onion, red peppers and green peppers into ¼" square pieces.

4 When the broth is almost evaporated, add the #3 vegetables and stir-fry briefly.

1 Cut the chicken into pieces.

4 Simmer #3 with the water.

2 Add the seasoning and salted shrimp to #1 and let stand.

3 Fry the chicken pieces lightly in a fry pan.

5 Add the round onion and red pepper slices and fry.

Salted Beef in Soy Sauce
Soegogi Changjorim (쇠고기 장조림)

Ingredients 1⅓ lb. brisket of beef, 6 cups water, ¾ cup soy sauce, 3 tbsp. sugar, 20 quail eggs, 4 red peppers, 4 Korean green peppers, 20 cloves garlic

Method **1** Cut the beef into 1⅔″ × 2″ pieces.
2 Boil the quail eggs for 7 minutes, rolling them so that the yolks will be centered, and peel.
3 Leave the stems on the peppers to a ⅓″ length.
4 Put enough water in a pan to cover the beef. Add the beef, bring to a hard boil and then simmer the beef on low heat.
5 When the meat is tender, add the garlic, soy sauce and sugar and simmer gently. Then add the #2, #3 ingredients and bring to a boil.
6 Shred the beef and halve the peppers to serve.

Hint You may use the shank of beef instead of the brisket of beef.

1 Cut the beef into 1⅔″ × 2″ pieces.

2 Boil the beef in the water.

3 Add the garlic, sugar and soy sauce and simmer.

4 Add the quail eggs and green peppers and boil briefly.

Potato and Beef in Soy Sauce
Soegogi Kamjajorim (쇠고기 감자조림)

Ingredients　1 oz. beef, green onion, garlic, sesame salt, 3 tbsp. soy sauce, 2 tbsp. sugar, ½ tbsp. sesame oil, pine nut powder, 2 potatoes, 1 cup water, Korean green peppers

Method　**1** Cut the peeled potatoes into chestnut-sized pieces rounding the edges into smooth oval shapes and wash.
2 Mince the beef finely and season it with the green onion, garlic, sesame salt, soy sauce, sugar and sesame oil. Stir-fry the beef and potatoes, add water and boil.
3 When the potatoes are almost cooked, add the green peppers and simmer on high heat.

4 Place in a serving dish and sprinkle with the powdered pine nuts.
Hint　To make the seasoning sauce for this food: Combine ½ cup soy sauce, rice wine, 2 tbsp. sugar, water and black pepper.

1 Cut the potatoes into chestnut-sized pieces and round off the edges.

3 Add 1 cup water to the fried ingredients and bring to a boil.

2 Stri-fry the seasoned beef and potatoes.

4 When the liquid is almost evaporated, add the green peppers and simmer on high heat until nicely glazed.

Rolled Beef with Vegetables in Soy Sauce
Soegogi Yach'aemarijorim (쇠고기 야채말이조림)

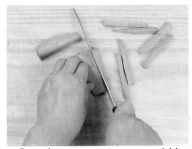

1 Cut the carrot into pencil-like pieces.

3 Wrap the vegetables in the beef slices and fasten.

5 Simmer the rolls on high heat until glazed.

2 Simmer the strips of burdock root with the seasoning.

4 Add the beef rolls to the boiling seasoning sauce.

Ingredients   **A** ¼ lb. beef, 1 tsp. rice wine, 1½ tsp. sugar, 2 tsp. soy sauce, 2 tsp. red pepper paste, 1 knob ginger, 4 tbsp. water
B ¼ burdock root, ¼ cup water, 1 tbsp. soy sauce, 1 tsp. sugar
C ¼ carrot, 3 green peppers
D ½ tomato, 5 lettuce leaves

Method   1 Cut the burdock root into pencil-like pieces. Scald and simmer with the **B** seasoning sauce.

2 Cut the carrot into the same size as the burdock root pieces and scald. Halve the green peppers to remove the seeds and cut them into thick strips.

3 Cut the beef into thin slices (about ⅛″). Wrap the green pepper, burdock root and carrot strips in the beef slice and fasten with a skewer. Simmer the A seasoning sauce until thick, add the beef rolls and cook them until the broth is almost evaporated.

4 Place the diagonally cut rolls on lettuce leaves on a plate and garnish with the tomato.

Hint   Scalded Angelica shoots can be used instead of the green peppers.

Beef and Bamboo Shoot in Soy Sauce
Soegogi Chuksunjangjorim （쇠고기 죽순장조림）

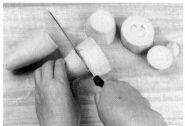

1 Cut the bamboo shoot into 2″ long chunks.

2 Scrape out the cores of the bamboo shoot chunks.

3 Cover the insides with flour and stuff them with the seasoned beef.

Ingredients   ½ lb. ground beef, 4 canned bamboo shoots, 1 tbsp. chopped green onion, 2 tsp. chopped garlic, 4 tbsp. flour, ½ tbsp. sesame salt, 1 tsp. sesame oil, 5 tbsp. soy sauce, 1 tbsp. sugar, ½ cup water, black pepper

Method   **1** Mix the ground beef with the green onion, garlic, black pepper and sesame oil.

2 Cut the bamboo shoot into 2″ long chunks.

3 Scrape out the cores of the bamboo shoot chunks and dust the insides with flour.

4 Stuff the **#3** bamboo shoots with the beef mixture. Then dip the stuffed chunks in flour.

5 Boil the soy sauce, sugar and water in a pan. When the seasoning sauce boils, add the **#4** stuffed chunks and simmer gently until glazed. Sprinkle with the sesame oil.

Hint   If fresh bamboo shoots (not canned) are used, scald them in boiling water to tenderize.

4 When the soy sauce, sugar and water boils, add the stuffed shoots and simmer until glazed.

Pork Meatballs in Soy Sauce
Twaejigogi Wanjajorim (돼지고기 완자조림)

Ingredients **A** ¼ lb. pork, 1 tsp. salt, ginger juice, ¼ round onion, 2 tbsp. cornstarch powder
B 10 Korean green peppers, ¼ lb. cabbage, ¼ carrot, salad oil
C ⅓ cup water, 1 tbsp. red pepper paste, 1 tbsp. rice wine, 1 tsp. soy sauce, 1 tsp. sugar

Method **1** Remove the stems from the long, Korean green peppers and cut them into ¾" lengths.
2 Mince the pork finely and mix it with the chopped round onion, cornstarch powder, 1 tsp. salt and ginger juice. Shape the mixture into meatballs ¾" in diameter. Roll the meatballs in cornstarch powder and deep-fry them in oil.
3 Bring the **C** seasoning to a boil, add the deep-fried meatballs and simmer. Then add the green peppers and cook briefly. Thread the meatballs and green peppers on skewers.
4 Arrange the skewered food around a centerpiece of cabbage strips and decorate the top with flower-shaped carrot pieces.
Hint This dish can be served for guests, or as a side dish for lunch boxes or an hors d'oeuvre.

1 Chop the round onion finely.

3 Mix the meat with the seasoning and cornstarch powder.

5 Deep-fry the meatballs in oil.

2 Fry the chopped round onion.

4 Roll the meatballs in cornstarch powder.

6 When the seasoning boils, add and simmer the deep-fried meatballs.

Spareribs in Sweet Sauce
Twaejigalbi Kangjöng (돼지갈비 강정)

Ingredients 1⅓ lb. pork ribs, black pepper, ginger juice, MSG, cornstarch powder, salad oil, 2 Korean green peppers, 2 red peppers, ¼ round onion, carrot, 2 cloves garlic, ¼ cup sweet sauce

Method 1 Remove excess fat from the spareribs. Boil them and then score and marinate them in the seasoning.

2 Halve the red peppers and green peppers to remove the seeds. Cut the peppers, carrot and round onion into flat pieces and fry them lightly in an oiled pan.

3 Dip the spareribs in cornstarch powder and deep-fry them in oil.

4 Place the deep-fried ribs, vegetables and sweet sauce in a pan and simmer together on low heat.

Hint 1 This is a high-grade dish which can be made easily for guests as a basic side dish if you prepare the sweet sauce beforehand.

2 To make the sweet sauce: 1 cup nicely aged soy sauce, ⅔ cup water, ½ lb. grain syrup (like dark corn syrup), 1 oz. ginger juice, ⅓ cup sugar, ¼ cup rice wine. Place the above ingredients in a pan and simmer them on low heat until thick.

Spareribs in Sweet Sauce

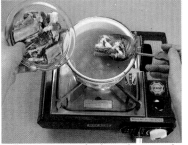

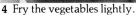

1 Remove excess fat from the spareribs and bring to a boil.

2 Slice the garlic, carrot and round onion into flat pieces.

4 Fry the vegetables lightly.

3 Dip the spareribs in cornstarch powder and deep-fry them in oil.

5 Add the sweet sauce and simmer.

Chicken in Soy Sauce
Takchorim (닭조림)

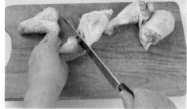

1 Cut the chicken into pieces.

2 Slice the carrot into large triangular pieces.

3 Fry the chicken pieces and remove the excess oil.

4 Add the seasoning sauce and water and simmer until glazed.

Ingredients   1 lb. chicken (half a chicken), 1 tbsp. oil, ½ carrot, 10 gingko nuts; 3 tbsp. soy sauce, 1½ tbsp. sugar, ginger juice, green onion, garlic, 1 cup water

Method   **1** Cut the chicken into pieces. Slice the carrot into large triangular pieces.

2 Fry the shelled gingko nuts in an oiled pan until they turn green.

3 Fry the carrot slightly. Fry the chicken pieces on high heat until golden brown.

4 Place the chicken, carrot, 1 cup water and half of the seasoning in a pan and simmer them on high heat for 10 minutes. When the liquid is almost evaporated, add the remaining seasoning and cook until glazed.

Deep-Fried Chicken in Soy Sauce
Takt'wigimjorim (닭뷔김조림)

Ingredients   1 lb. chicken, 1 tbsp. rice wine, 1 tbsp. soy sauce, 1 green onion, 1 knob ginger, 1 cup cornstarch powder, ½ round onion, 2 Korean green peppers, ½ carrot, 2 cloves garlic, ⅓ cup sweet sauce, 2 oz. cabbage, ½ cucumber, 4 olive, tomato

Method   **1** Halve the whole chicken. Sprinkle the chicken with the rice wine and soy sauce and top it with the sliced ginger and round onion and steam it in a steamer.

2 Cut the steamed chicken into pieces. Dip them in flour and deep-fry them in oil.

3 Cut the round onion and green peppers into large pieces. Cut the carrot into crescent-shaped pieces and the garlic in flat pieces.

4 Fry the **#3** vegetables in an oiled pan. Add the chicken and sweet sauce and simmer until glazed.

5 Place the cabbage, cucumber and carrot cut into thin strips in a glassware dish and garnish with the olives and tomato. Serve this salad with the chicken.

Hint   To make the sweet sauce: Combine 1 cup nicely aged soy sauce, ½ lb. grain syrup (like dark corn syrup), ⅓ cup sugar, ⅔ cup water, 1 oz. ginger cut in flat pieces, ¼ cup rice wine, 1 tsp. black pepper, and MSG in a pan and simmer on low heat until thick.

1 Top the seasoned chicken with the sliced ginger and onion and steam.

3 Deep-fry the chicken pieces in oil until brown.

5 Fry the garlic and **#4** vegetables in an oiled pan.

2 Cut the steamed chicken into pieces and dip them in flour.

4 Slice the vegetables into big pieces.

6 Cook all the ingredients with the sweet sauce.

Broiled Foods
Deep-Fat Fried Foods

Barbecued Beef
Pulgogi (불고기)

Ingredients   1⅓ lb. top round or tenderloin of beef, 3 tbsp. sugar, 2 tbsp. rice wine, 5 tbsp. chopped green onion, 2 tbsp. chopped garlic, 6 tbsp. soy sauce, 1 tbsp. sesame salt, 2 tbsp. sesame oil, black pepper, MSG, lettuce, garland chrysanthemum, sesame leaves, garlic, small green onions

Method   **1** Slice the beef thinly and score lightly with a knife to make it more tender. Cut it into bite-sized pieces and marinate it in the sugar and rice wine.
2 Mix the marinated beef thoroughly with the soy sauce, chopped garlic, sesame salt, MSG and sesame oil.
3 Broil the seasoned beef over hot charcoal on a grill or in a fry pan. Pulgogi is delicious served with lettuce leaves, sesame leaves, garland chrysanthemum and garlic.

Hint   **1** Cut the beef against the grain to make it tender.
2 Pulgogi is generally broiled over charcoal on a grill at the table. Otherwise, you may use an oven-broiler heated to 570°F for 10 minutes.

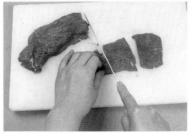

1 Slice the beef thinly and cut into bite-sized pieces.

2 Marinate the #1 beef in the sugar and rice wine.

3 Add the seasoning sauce and mix well.

4 Broil the seasoned beef over hot charcoal.

Broil pulgogi over hot charcoal on a grill.

Broiled Beef Ribs
Soegalbigui (쇠갈비구이)

1 Score the meaty parts of the ribs taking care not to cut the bones.

2 Flatten the rib meat and score deeply.

Ingredients 4 lb. beef ribs, garlic, 6 tbsp. rice wine, 5 tbsp. sugar, 9 tbsp. chopped green onion, 3 tbsp. soy sauce, chopped garlic, 6 tbsp. sesame salt, 6 tbsp. sesame oil, lettuce leaves, green onion strips, round onion, pine nuts

Method **1** Clean the ribs. Score the meaty parts of ribs taking care not to cut the bones. Flatten the rib meat, score deeply and place them in a bowl.

2 Sprinkle the ribs with the sugar and rice wine and mix well.

3 Mix the soy sauce with the chopped green onion, garlic, sesame salt and sesame oil to make the seasoning sauce.

4 Add the seasoning sauce to the #2 ribs and let them stand for 1 hour.

5 Place the ribs on a hot grill and broil turning them several times.

3 Add the seasoning sauce to the ribs and mix well.

4 Broil the ribs on a hot grill.

Broiled Beef Intestine in Salt
Kopch'ang Sogŭmgui (곰창 소금구이)

1 Remove excess fat from the small intestine with a scissors.

2 Cut the small intestine into 4″ lengths.

3 Clean the small intestine by rubbing it with salt.

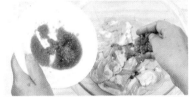

4 Season the small intestine with the sesame oil, salt and black pepper.

Ingredients 1⅓ lb. small beef intestine, 2 tbsp. salt, 1 large green onion, 10 cloves garlic, 2 tbsp. sesame oil, black pepper, MSG, lettuce leaves, garland chrysanthemum, 2 red peppers

Method **1** Remove excess fat from the small intestine and cut it into 4″ lengths. Rub the small intestine with salt, wash and drain well.

2 Score the trimmed small intestine in various places.

3 Peel and clean the garlic. Cut the red peppers into small rings.

4 Season the small intestine with the sesame oil, black pepper, MSG and salt and mix well.

5 Place the small intestine pieces on a hot oiled grill and broil them evenly turning often.

6 Put the garlic cloves on the edge of a grill and cook gently.

7 When cooked, place the small intestine pieces on lettuce leaves on a plate and serve with the garlic, black pepper, salt, sesame salt and red pepper.

Hint Broil this food on high heat for top flavor. Otherwise, the meat juice is lost and the small intestine becomes hard too quickly.

1 Sprinkle the pork with the ginger juice and mix well.

2 Add the seasoning sauce to **#1**, mix well and let it stand.

Ingredients 1⅓ lb. pork (with fat and skin remaining), 4 tbsp.

3 Brush the hot grill with sesame oil.

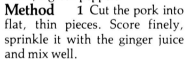

4 Broil the seasoned pork on the hot grill.

soy sauce, 1 tbsp. salted soused shrimp, 3 tbsp. sugar, 1 tbsp. ginger juice, small green onion, 10 cloves garlic, 2 tbsp. sesame salt, 2 tbsp. sesame oil, black pepper, MSG, 3 green peppers

Method **1** Cut the pork into flat, thin pieces. Score finely, sprinkle it with the ginger juice and mix well.

2 Combine the soy sauce, salted soused shrimp, sugar, chopped garlic, chopped green onion, sesame salt, sesame oil, black pepper and MSG to make the seasoning sauce.

3 Mix the pork with the seasoning sauce and let it stand.

4 Place the seasoned pork pieces on a hot oiled grill and broil them turning often.

Hint Pork tastes best when cooked thoroughly.

Broiled Pork Spareribs
Twaejigalbigui (돼지갈비구이)

Ingredients 2⅔ lb. pork spareribs, 6 tbsp. soy sauce, black pepper, 4 tbsp. sugar, 6 tbsp. chopped green onion, 2 tbsp. chopped garlic, 1 tbsp. ginger juice, 2 tbsp. sesame salt, 2 tbsp. sesame oil, 2 Korean green peppers, 1 red pepper, 1 round onion, MSG, 6 skewers

Method **1** Cut the spareribs into 2¾" lengths and score them lightly at ⅓" intervals. Sprinkle the ribs with the ginger juice, 2 tbsp. sugar and mix well.

2 Combine the soy sauce, sugar, chopped green onion, chopped garlic, sesame salt, sesame oil, black pepper and MSG to make the seasoning sauce.

3 Add the seasoning sauce to the ribs and rub it in with your hands, so that the ribs are well coated with the seasoning.

4 Place the spareribs on a hot oiled grill and broil them by turning often. Be careful so that the seasoning does not get scorched and fall off the ribs.

5 Serve the broiled spareribs topped with the sliced lemon.

Hint Marinate the pork in the ginger juice and broil it basting with the seasoning sauce.

1 Cut the spareribs into 2¾" lengths and score them a ⅓" intervals.

2 Add the ginger juice and sugar and rub it in.

3 Sprinkle the #2 ribs with the seasoning sauce and let them stand.

4 Broil the spareribs with the small green onion and garlic on a hot grill.

Hot Broiled Pork
Twaejigogi Koch'ujanggui (돼지고기 고추장구이)

Ingredients   1⅓ lb. pork, 2 tbsp. chopped garlic, 3 tbsp. chopped green onion, 4 tbsp. red pepper paste, 2 tbsp. sugar, 1 tbsp. sesame salt, 1 tbsp. sesame oil, 1 tbsp. ginger juice, black pepper, MSG, lettuce leaves, small green onion, sesame leaves, 10 cloves garlic

Method   **1** Use lean pork; slice it thinly and score it finely. Sprinkle the pork with the ginger juice and mix well.

2 Combine the red pepper paste, soy sauce, chopped green onion, garlic, sesame salt, sesame oil, sugar, black pepper and MSG to make the seasoned red pepper paste.

3 Add the seasoned red pepper paste to the meat and rub it in.

4 Place the seasoned meat on a hot grill and broil on medium heat.

5 Place the hot broiled meat on a plate and serve with the lettuce leaves, sesame leaves, small green onion, garlic and stuffed cucumber kimchi.

Hint   Sprinkling the pork with ginger juice removes any odor; broil for a tasty dish.

1 Slice the pork thinly.

2 Score the sliced pork lightly.

3 Add the ginger juice to #2.

4 Add the seasoned red pepper paste to the meat and rub it in.

5 Oil the grill.

6 Broil the meat on direct heat first and then cook on medium heat.

51

Baked Whole Chicken
T'ongdakkui (통닭구이)

1 Sprinkle the clean chicken with the salt, black pepper and ginger juice.

3 Turn the wings backward and twist the legs.

4 Layer the vegetables in the bottom, then put the chicken on them and put the remaining vegetables on top.

2 Cut the rear part of the neck and fasten it in the back of the chicken with a toothpick.

5 Bake the chicken for 40 minutes.

Ingredients   1 whole chicken, 1 tsp. salt, ¾ oz. butter, 1 round onion, ½ carrot, ½ cup sweet soy sauce, 1 knob ginger, parsley, 1 tomato, ribbon

Method   **1** Clean the whole chicken and sprinkle it with the salt, black pepper and ginger juice.
2 Cut the round onion and carrot into thin strips. Layer half of the vegetables on the bottom of the oven pan, then place the chicken on these vegetables and layer the remaining vegetables on top of the chicken.
3 Bake the chicken for 10 minutes in an oven.
4 Remove the vegetables from the chicken and bake for 10 minutes more. Then baste it with the sweet soy sauce and bake it for 20 minutes more.
5 Wrap the legs of the chicken with foil and tie the ribbon on the neck. Garnish with the tomato and parsley.

Deep-Fried Beef
Soegogit'wigim (쇠고기튀김)

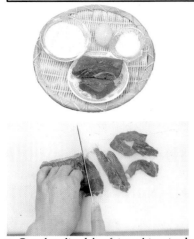

Ingredients   1 lb. beef, 1 cup cornstarch powder, 1 egg, salad oil, black pepper, MSG, 2 oz. Chinese noodles, 1 tsp. salt, parsley

Method   **1** Trim the lean beef and slice it thinly.

2 Cut the sliced beef into bite-sized pieces. Mix the beef pieces with the salt, black pepper, MSG and beaten egg well and dip them in cornstarch powder.

3 Heat the oil in a deep-fry pan and when smoking, add the meat pieces and deep-fry them until golden brown; after few minutes fry them once more.

4 Deep-fry the Chinese noodles and spread them on a plate. Serve the deep-fried beef with kimchi and garnish with the parsley.

Hint   When you deep-fry the beef, do not put too many beef pieces in the hot oil. The oil temperature falls if you add too many at a time.

1 Cut the sliced beef into bite-sized pieces.

2 Mix the beef with the salt, black pepper, MSG and beaten egg.

3 Dip the seasoned meat in the cornstarch powder.

4 Deep-fry the beef pieces twice.

Deep-Fried Beef and Gingko Nuts
Soegogi Samsaegunhaengt'wigim (쇠고기 삼색은행튀김)

Ingredients   ⅔ lb. beef, ½ cup gingko nuts, 2 round onions, 1 carrot, 5 green peppers, 1 tbsp. salt, ½ cup cornstarch powder, black pepper, MSG, 10 skewers, parsley

Method   1 Choose tender, lean beef and cut it into ½" square pieces. Score finely and sprinkle with salt and black pepper.
2 Cut the carrot and round onions into the same size as the beef pieces.
3 Fry the shelled gingko nuts until green and peel off the top-skin.
4 Halve the green peppers to remove the seeds and cut them into ½" square pieces.

5 Season the above ingredients with salt, black pepper and MSG.
6 Skewer the beef, carrot, round onion, green pepper pieces and ginko nuts alternating the colors.
7 Sprinkle the cornstarch powder over the skewered food.
8 Heat the oil to 360°F in a pan and deep-fry two or three skewers of food at a time. Deep-fry them once again after a few minutes.
9 Drain on absorbent paper, place the deep-fried food on a plate and garnish with the parsley.

1 Cut the round onions, carrot and green   peppers into ½" square pieces.

3 Skewer the prepared ingredients.

4 Sprinkle the constarch powder over the skewered food.

2 Stir-fry the gingko nuts and remove the inner skin.

5 Deep-fry the skewered food in oil.

Deep-Fried Beef Rolled in Sesame Leaves
Soegogi Kkaennipmarit'wigim (쇠고기 깻잎말이튀김)

1 Mix and season the mashed bean curd and minced beef.

2 Clean the sesame leaves and dry off the moisture. Then dip the insides into flour.

3 Place a spoonful of the meat mixture on a sesame leaf and roll it up.

4 Stick the skewers into the rolls to fasten.

5 Dip the rolls into flour and then into beaten egg and deep-fry them in boiling oil.

Ingredients ⅔ lb. beef, 10 sesame leaves, ½ cake bean curd, 1 egg, ½ cup flour, 2 tbsp. chopped green onion, 1 tbsp. chopped garlic, 2 tsp. sesame salt, 2 tsp. sesame oil, 1 tbsp. salt, black pepper, MSG, 10 small skewers, ½ cucumber, 2 bundles parsley, 1 red radish

Method **1** Slice the beef thinly and mince well.

2 Wrap the bean curd in a clean cloth, squeeze out the excess water and mash it finely.

3 Combine the meat, bean curd, chopped green onion, garlic, sesame salt, sesame oil, black pepper, MSG and salt and mix well.

4 Wash the sesame leaves and dry off the moisture.

5 Dip the insides of sesame leaves in flour. Place the spoonful of the meat mixture on each leaf and roll it up and fasten with a small skewer.

6 Dip the rolls into flour and then into beaten egg and deep-fry them in boiling oil.

7 Drain and arrange the cucumber cut into thin rings and diagonally cut rolls in the center of a plate. Garnish with the parsley and red radish.

Hint Deep-fry the food in very hot oil until crisp. To drain stand the deep-fried food on end, so that it does not become soft.

Deep-Fried Chicken Legs
Taktarit'wigim (닭다리튀김)

Ingredients   6 chicken legs, 1 tbsp. ginger juice, ½ tbsp. salt, 1 egg, ½ cup cornstarch powder, black pepper, MSG, frying oil, parsley, red radish

Method   **1** Loosen the meat from the bones being careful to leave it attached at the lower end. Score the meat to tenderize and sprinkle it with the ginger juice, black pepper, MSG and salt rubbing the seasonings in.

2 Pour the beaten egg evenly over the meat.

3 Dip the chicken legs into the cornstarch powder and deep-fry them twice in boiling oil.

4 Place the deep-fried chicken legs on a plate and garnish with the parsley and red radish.

Hint   Place the cucumber, carrot, cabbage and boiled egg white cut into thin strips in a bowl and sprinkle the sieved egg yolk on top. Serve the deep-fried chicken legs with these vegetables.

1 Loosen the meat from the bones, leaving the lower ends attached.

2 Sprinkle with the salt, ginger juice and black pepper and mix well.

3 Pour the beaten egg evenly over the meat.

4 Dip the legs into the cornstarch powder and deep-fry them in oil.

Pan-Fried Foods
Skewered Foods

Fried Pork in Egg Batter
Tonjŏn (돈전)

1 Wrap the bean curd in a cloth, squeeze out the water and mash it.

2 Mix the minced pork, kimchi and bean curd with the seasoning well.

3 Oil your hands and shape the mixture into round, flat patties.

patties.

4 Dip the patties into flour, then into beaten egg and fry them until golden brown. Garnish with the parsley and green onion cut into thin strips.

Hint **1** Season the kimchi and bean curd and mix them thoroughly with a flat wooden spoon or with your hands so that the patties will be nicely shaped. You may use parboiled mung bean sprouts instead of the kimchi. When draining the fried food in a wicker tray, make only one layer.

2 Be sure to remove all the fat from the pork as it may otherwise be too greasy. Also, cook the pork well.

Ingredients ½ lb. ground pork, 1 cake bean curd, ½ cup flour, 2 cloves garlic, 1 large green onion, ¼ lb. kimchi, parsley, sesame oil, 2 eggs, salt, black pepper, MSG, 1 tsp. ginger juice

Method **1** Wrap the bean curd in a cloth, squeeze out the water and mash it.

2 Squeeze out the water from the kimchi. Chop the kimchi and green onion finely.

3 Mix the **#1, #2** ingredients, ground pork, garlic, salt, black pepper, sesame oil and MSG and shape the mixture into round, flat

Fried Liver in Egg Batter
Kanjŏn (간전)

Ingredients ⅔ lb. liver, 1 egg, ½ cup flour, salt, black pepper, lemon, olive

Method **1** Remove the membrane from the liver and rinse to remove any blood.
2 Slice the liver thinly and score and sprinkle it with the salt and black pepper.
3 Dip the liver into flour and then into beaten egg.
4 Fry the liver in a moderately hot oiled pan until golden brown and garnish with the lemon and olive.

Hint **1** Soak the liver in water to remove any blood; otherwise the fried liver becomes black.
2 Score the liver; otherwise the fried liver will curl up.

1 Remove the membrane from the liver and rinse it to remove any blood.

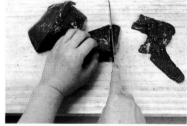

2 Slice the liver and score it lightly.

3 Sprinkle the liver slices with the salt and black pepper.

4 Dip the liver slices into flour and then into beaten egg and fry them until golden brown.

Skewered Beef
Soegogi Sanjŏk (쇠고기 산적)

1 Cut the beef into 3″ long and ¼″ thick strips.

3 Marinate the meat in the seasoning sauce.

A grill may be used for broiling the skewered food.

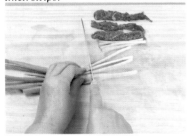

2 Cut the small green onions into lengths shorter than the meat strips.

4 String the meat and small green onion strips alternately on skewers.

5 Fry the skewered food in an oiled pan.

Ingredients   ½ lb. beef, ¼ lb. small green onion, seasoning sauce: (1 tbsp. sugar, 2 tsp. rice wine, 2 tbsp. soy sauce, 2 large green onions, 3 cloves garlic, 1 tbsp. sesame salt, 2 tsp. sesame oil), salad oil

Method   **1** Select lean beef and cut it into thin slices about ¼″ thick.
2 Score the beef slices to tenderize and cut them into 3″ long, pencil-wide strips.
3 Trim the small green onions and cut them into lengths slightly shorter than the beef strips.
4 Marinate the beef in the seasoning sauce.
5 Trim the wooden or bamboo skewers with a knife and rinse them in water.
6 String the seasoned meat and small green onion strips alternately on skewers and beginning and ending with the meat. Then baste the filled skewers with the seasoning sauce.
7 Fry the skewered food in a hot oiled pan until the meat is browned on both sides.

Hint   **1** Cut the meat into strips longer than the vegetables, as the meat shrinks when cooked.
2 When you string the food on skewers, stick the skewers into the upper part of the food.

Skewered Pork and Kimchi
Twaejigogi Kimch'isanjŏk (돼지고기 김치산적)

1 Cut the pork into ⅓″×3½″ strips and pound them with the back of knife.

2 Season the pork with the ginger, garlic, soy sauce, sugar and green onions.

3 Squeeze out the water from the kimchi and season.

Ingredients   ½ lb. pork, ½ lb. kimchi, 1 tbsp. sugar, 2 tsp. sesame oil, 10 small green onions, ½ cup flour, 1 egg, various seasonings, parsley, red radish

Method   **1** Cut the pork into ⅓″×3½″ strips and pound the pork strips with the back of knife to tenderize them. Marinate them in the seasoning sauce.

2 Cut the kimchi into 3″ lengths and squeeze out the water. Season it with the sesame oil and sugar.

3 Cut the small green onions into 3″ lengths.

4 String the pork, kimchi and green onion strips alternately on skewers. Dip one side of the skewered food into flour.

5 Dip the **#4** skewered food into beaten egg and fry it until golden brown.

6 Garnish with the parsley and red radish and serve with the seasoning sauce for dipping.

Hint   A tasty variation is angelica shoots instead of kimchi.

4 String the pork, kimchi, and small green onions alternately on skewers.

5 Dip one side of the **#4** skewered food into flour.

6 Dip the skewered food into beaten egg and fry.

Broiled Chicken Patty
Takkogi Sopsanjŏk (닭고기 섭산적)

Ingredients 1 spring chicken, 4 tbsp. chopped green onion, 2 tbsp. chopped garlic, 1 tbsp. chopped ginger, 1 tbsp. sesame salt, 2 tbsp. sesame oil, ½ tsp. salt, 3 tbsp. soy sauce, black pepper, red pepper thread, lettuce, cucumber

Method **1** Remove the meat from the bones and mince it finely.

2 Add the seasoning sauce to the minced meat and mix well. Shape the mixture into round flat patties.

3 Broil the patties in a hot oiled pan or on a grill, taking care not to burn them. (Or, you may fry them in an oiled pan on medium heat.)

Hint Mince all the ingredients finely and mix them thoroughly,

so that the patties keep a nice shape. This dish is especially good for students' lunch boxes.

1 Remove the meat from the bones and mince it finely.

3 Shape the **#2** mixture into round flat patties on an oiled kitchen board.

2 Add the seasoning sauce and mix well.

4 Pan-broil the patties until brown.

Skewered Beef with Vegetables
Chapsanjŏk (잡산적)

Ingredients ¼ lb. beef, ¼ lb. bellflower roots, 10 small green onions, 2 oz. bracken (fern shoots), ½ carrot, 5 dried brown, oak mushrooms, seasoning sauce: (3 tbsp. soy sauce, 1 tsp. sesame salt, 1 tbsp. green onion, ½ tbsp. garlic, sesame oil, black pepper, MSG), skewers

Method 1 Cut the beef into thin slices about ¼" thick. Score the slices evenly and cut them into ⅓" × 3" strips.

2 Soak the bellflower roots to remove the bitterness. Scald in boiling water, cut into 2¾" long pencil-wide strips and pound them with the back of knife to tenderize.

3 Trim the small green onions and dried mushrooms and cut them into 2¾" long strips.

4 Cut the bracken and carrot into 2¾" long pencil-wide strips and scald them slightly.

5 Make the seasoning sauce.

6 Marinate the beef in one-third of the seasoning sauce for 20 minutes.

7 Mix the carrot, bracken, small green onion and bellflower roots with the seasoning sauce.

8 String the above ingredients on skewers alternating the colors and fry them in a fry pan.

1 Cut the beef into ¼" thick and ⅓" × 3" strips.

2 Cut the carrot, dried mushrooms, bracken and bellflower roots into 2¾" long pencil-wide strips.

3 Mix the beef and vegetables with the seasoning sauce.

4 Skewer the ingredients alternating the colors and fry

Skewered Boiled Beef
Hwayangjŏk (화양적)

Ingredients ⅓ lb. pressed meat, 6 dried brown, oak mushrooms, 5 bellflower roots, 1 cucumber, 2 carrots, 2 eggs, 1 tbsp. chopped pine nuts, ½ tbsp. sesame salt, 1 tsp. sesame oil, 1 tbsp. chopped green onion, 1 tbsp. chopped garlic, ½ tbsp. sugar, black pepper, red radish, 2 tbsp. soy sauce

Method **1** To make the pressed meat: Boil the beef or the pork. Wrap the boiled meat in a cloth and press it with a heavy weight. When the meat is cooled, slice it into strips 2⅓″ long and ¼″ thick. **2** Soak the dried mushrooms in water and remove the stems. Slice them into 2⅓″ lengths.

3 Shred the bellflower roots into strips ¼″ thick. Cut the carrot into strips 2⅓″ long and ¼″ thick. Scald them in boiling water.

4 Choose a thin, tender cucumber and cut it into strips 2⅓″ long and

¼" thick. Sprinkle with salt.

5 Separate the whites and yolks of eggs and beat gently. Mix the beaten egg whites, and also the yolks with 1 tbsp. cornstarch flour, 1 tbsp. water and salt each. Fry these mixtures in a square pan in thick sheets and let them cool. Cut the egg sheets into strips 2⅓" long.

6 Season all the ingredients except the egg strips with the soy sauce, sesame salt, black pepper, sesame oil, green onion and chopped garlic and fry lightly.

7 String the ingredients on skewers alternating the colors. Sprinkle the top with powdered pine nuts on a plate. Garnish with red radish and parsley.

Hint Bellflower root is a tasty addition to this dish. It is an alkaline food containing sugar, fiber, calcium and iron.

1 Cut the pressed meat into strips ⅓" × 2⅓".

2 Cut the vegetables into the same size strips as the meat.

3 Season and fry the #1 meat and #2 vegetable strips lightly.

4 Skewer the ingredients alternating the colors.

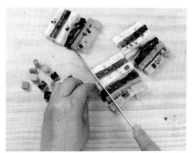

5 Trim the edges making uniformly sized servings.

Skewered Rice Cake
Ttoksanjŏk (떡산적)

Ingredients 3 rolls of rice cake, ⅓ lb. beef, 1 carrot, 10 small green onions, 6 dried brown, oak mushrooms, 3 tbsp. soy sauce, 2 large green onions, 3 cloves garlic, 1 tbsp. sesame oil, 2 tbsp. sesame salt, 2 tsp. sugar, black pepper, red pepper threads, 10 skewers

Method 1 Cut the rolls of rice cake into 2¾" lengths and quarter them lengthwise. Scald and rinse in cold water.

2 Score the beef lightly and cut it into 3" long, pencil-wide strips.

3 Cut the carrot into 2¾" long, pencil-wide strips and scald them in boiling water.

4 Trim and cut the small green onions into 2¾" lengths.

5 Soak the dried mushrooms, remove the stems and cut the mushrooms into ⅓" wide, 2¾" long strips.

6 Chop the green onions and garlic finely.

7 Combine the soy sauce, green onion, garlic, sesame oil, sesame salt, black pepper and sugar to make the seasoning sauce.

8 Mix the prepared ingredients with half of the seasoning sauce.

9 String the seasoned ingredients on skewers alternating the colors beginning and ending with the rice cakes.

10 Baste both sides of the skewered food with the remaining seasoning sauce and fry them in an oiled pan or broil them on a grill.

Hint 1 When the rice cake hardens a little, you can cut it into pretty shapes. If the rice cake becomes too hard, cut it and then scald and rinse in cold water before frying.

2 Trim both edges of the skewered food, so that it looks neat.

1 Cut the rolls of rice cake into 2¾" lengths and quarter them

2 Scald the rice cake in boiling water and rinse in cold water.

3 Fry the skewered food basting with the seasoning sauce.

66

Raw Meats
Pressed Meats

Raw Meat
Yuk'oe (육회)

Ingredients ⅔ lb. beef, 2½ tbsp. soy sauce, 1½ tbsp. sugar, 1 tbsp. chopped green onion, 2 tsp. chopped garlic, 1 tbsp. sesame salt, 2 tbsp. sesame oil, 1 crisp Korean pear, 2 tbsp. pine nut powder, 4 lettuce leaves, 1 egg yolk

Method **1** Select fresh, lean beef. Slice thinly and cut again into thin strips; mix with the seasoning sauce.
2 Peel the Korean pear and cut it into thin strips. Soak it in sugar water for a while and drain.
3 Heap the beef strips on the lettuce leaves in the center of the plate with the pear strips on the side.
4 Put the egg yolk on top of the meat and sprinkle it with powdered pine nuts.
Hint You must use only very fresh beef of good quality because it is being eaten raw.

1 Slice the beef thinly and cut it into thin strips.

4 Soak the pear in sugar water and drain.

2 Mix the beef strips with the seasoning sauce.

5 Place the pear and beef strips on the lettuce leaves.

3 Peel the pear and cut it into thin strips.

6 Put the egg yolk on top of the beef.

Sliced Raw Liver and Tripe

Kan · Ch'ŏnyŏp'oe (간 · 처녑회)

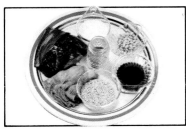

Ingredients   ½ lb. liver, ⅔ lb. tripe, 5 tbsp. pine nuts, 3 tbsp. sesame oil, 1 tbsp. salt, black pepper, sesame salt, lettuce leaves

Method   **1** Remove the membrane from the liver and slice it thinly. Then rub it lightly with salt and rinse it in running water to remove any blood.

2 Rub half of the tripe with salt and rinse it in water. Parboil in boiling water, rinse it in cold water and remove the skin.

3 Rub the remaining tripe with salt and clean it to remove the scent.

4 Cut the liver and tripe into ¾″ wide and 2″ long slices. Put a pine nut on each slice and roll it up.

5 Arrange the liver and tripe rolls on lettuce leaves on a plate.

6 Serve with sesame oil, black pepper, sesame salt and salt.

Hint   **1** Though you can eat raw tripe, it is safer to eat slightly scalded tripe.

2 Scald the tripe only briefly for easier removal of the skin.

1 Remove the membrane from the liver.

2 Rub the tripe with salt and rinse it to remove the scent.

3 Scald half of the tripe in boiling water and skin it.

4 Put a pine nut at the end of each slice of liver and tripe and roll firmly.

Cold Cooked Chicken and Vegetables
Takkogi Naengch'ae (닭고기 냉채)

Ingredients　1 lb. chicken, ½ lb. jellyfish, 1 carrot, 1 cucumber, 1 pear, 2 eggs, mustard sauce: (7 tbsp. mustard powder, 3 tbsp. sugar, 2 tbsp. salt, 1 tbsp. soy sauce, ½ cup water, ½ cup vinegar), chopped stone mushrooms

Method　**1** Clean the chicken well and baste it with the soy sauce. Deep-fry the chicken in oil and cut the meat into thick strips.
2 Separate the egg yolk and egg white. Fry the yolk into a thin sheet. Mix the egg white with the chopped stone mushrooms and fry in a thin sheet.
3 Cut the egg sheets, carrot and cucumber into flat rectangles.

4 Scald the jellyfish briefly in warm water (140° F). Then cut it into 2⅓″ long strips and mix it with the sugar and vinegar.
5 Cut one-third of the prepared cucumber pieces into thin strips.
6 Arrange the flat pieces of carrot, cucumber, egg white and egg yolk around the edge of a plate. Pile the sliced chicken in the center and ring it with the jellyfish and cucumber strips.
7 Serve with ½ cup of the mustard sauce.

Hint　If you fry the chicken basted with the soy sauce, the color becomes a lovely brown, but if you steam the chicken instead, it tastes especially delicious.

1 Cut the fried chicken into thick strips.

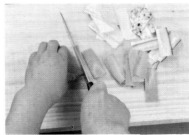

2 Cut the carrot, egg sheets and cucumber into flat pieces.

3 Mix the jellyfish strips with the vinegar and sugar.

Pressed Boiled Beef
Soegogisaťae P'yŏnyuk (쇠고기사태 편육)

Ingredients **A** 1⅓ lb. shank of beef, ½ round onion, ½ carrot, lettuce leaves

B 5 tbsp. soy sauce, 2 tbsp. vinegar, 2 tbsp. chopped green onion, 1 tbsp. chopped garlic, 1 tsp. sugar, black pepper, sesame salt

Method **1** Clean the shank of beef.

2 Cut the round onion and carrot into thin strips.

3 Boil the shank of beef with the round onion and carrot.

4 Take the meat out of the pot and wrap it in a cloth and press it with a heavy weight.

5 When the meat becomes firm, cut it into thin slices. Arrange the sliced meat on lettuce leaves on a plate.

6 Make the seasoning sauce with the **B** ingredients and serve. .

1 Cut the round onion and carrot into thin strips.

3 When the meat is well-done, drain it and wrap it in a cloth.

2 Boil the shank of beef and #1 vegetables.

4 Press the meat with a heavy weight.

Pressed Boiled Pork
Twaejigogi P'yŏnyuk (돼지고기 편육)

Ingredients   1⅓ lb. pork, 2 tbsp. soybean paste, 2 knobs ginger, ½ lb. kimchi, tiny soused salted shrimp seasoning: (4 tbsp. salted shrimp juice, 2 tbsp. chopped green onion, 1 tsp. chopped garlic, sesame salt, 1 tbsp. red pepper powder, black pepper, sesame oil, water), lettuce leaves

Method   **1** Wash the pork in cold water, cut it into large pieces and tie them together tightly with string.

2 Slice the ginger thinly.

3 Dissolve and boil the soybean paste in water. Add the meat and ginger when boiling and simmer until tender.

4 Remove the excess fat and froth which have floated to the top.

5 When the meat is well-done, drain and rinse in cold water, wrap in a cloth and press it with a heavy weight.

6 When the meat becomes firm, cut it into thin slices. Arrange the sliced meat on lettuce leaves on a plate and serve with the kimchi.

7 Mix the salted shrimps with the seasoning and serve. Add some water if the soused shrimp is too salty.

Hint   Pressed boiled pork is very tasty served with garland chrysanthemum, green pepper or vinegar-red pepper sauce.

1 Boil the pork and sliced ginger.

2 Remove excess fat and froth from the top.

3 Wrap the meat in a cloth and press it with a heavy weight.

4 Add the seasoning to the tiny soused salted shrimp.

GLOSSARY

Angelica Shoots (turŭp) are young shoots with tender green leaves of the angelica bush which are available fresh only in early spring.

Bamboo Shoots (chuksun) are the tender spring sprouts of the bamboo, off-white in color and shaped like a bud. Their flesh is tender but firm and should be scalded about 5 minutes in boiling water if used fresh.

Barley Tea (porich'a) is tea made from toasted barley kernels. It is prepared by adding the toasted barley to boiling water, boiling for 5 minutes, straining and serving. Barley tea is served cooled in the summer and warm in the winter. Corn tea is prepared and served the same way but is made from parched corn kernels.

Bean Curd (tubu) is a square or rectangular cake of pressed, coagulated soybean puree—the "cheese" of soymilk. It has a bland texture and is a very easy-to-digest, nutritious food. It should be kept in water (changing water daily) in the refrigerator.

Beans: There are a large variety of dried beans available in the Korean grain-bean shops. In addition there are various processed bean foods also available for daily use in the Korean diet.

— yellow soybeans (hŭink'ong), sprouts (k'ongnamul), bean curd (tubu), soft bean curd (sundubu), bean paste (toenjang), fermented soybeans for making soy sauce (meju), seasoned fermented soybeans (ch'ŏnggukchang), soybean flour (k'ongkaru), soy sauce (kanjang).

— Brown soybeans (pamk'ong—literally "chestnut beans") are a chestnut brown color and have a smooth chestnut-like texture when cooked.

— Black soybeans (kŏmŭnk'ong) are served as a side dish.

— mung beans (noktu), sprouts (sukchu namul), jellied mung bean puree (ch'ŏngp'o), mung bean flour (noktu karu).

— red kidney beans (kangnamk'ong)

Bean Sprouts (k'ongnamul) may be grown at home, if desired, in a warm, wet jar or purchased in most vegetable sections of grocery stores. The large sprouts are from the yellow soybean; the smaller more delicate sprouts are from the green mung bean.

Bellflower Root (toraji) is a white root from the mountainside bellflower.

Bracken (kosari) is the early spring shoot of the fern plant. These shoots are gathered in the spring and sold fresh at that time. They are also dried for re-hydration later in the year. There is a common variety and a rather special royal fern variety that has larger, softer shoots.

Burdock Root (uŏng) is a long, fat nutritious root with a distinctive flavor which is washed, scrubbed and scraped, soaked in vinegar-water so that it does not change color and then cut into thick strips for use.

Chinese Cabbage (paech'u) is a solid, oblong head of wide stalk-leaves with a subtle flavor used widely in making kimchi.

Chinese Noodles (tangmyŏn) are very thin transparent noodles made from mung bean flour. They are sold dried in long loops. They should be soaked in warm water before use and cooked quickly. When cooked they become opaque and slippery.

Cinnamon (kyep'i) is a rough brown bark. It can be used whole or dried and ground to use in seasoning.

Eggplant (kaji) is the long, purple, shiny fruit of the eggplant plant; it is not large and round but sleek and elongated with a slight bulbousness at the end opposite the stem.

Garland Chrysanthemum (ssukkat) is a pungent, edible variety of Chrysanthemum; the leaves are used for seasoning and decorating like lettuce leaves in Korean recipes.

Garlic (manŭl), related to the onion, has a bulb made up of several cloves with a strong odor and flavor. It is widely used as seasoning in Korean dishes after being finely chopped. Garlic is also served pickled and its long green stems are eaten raw or boiled.

Ginger Root (saenggang) adds zip to many Korean dishes. Fresh ginger root has a thin light-brown skin over knobby bulbs. It may be washed and dried and placed in the freezer in a plastic bag. It is then available for grating into whatever dish is being prepared. It may be dried and powdered but fresh ginger is called for in most Korean recipes.

Gingko Nuts (ŭnhaeng) are oval-shaped, yellowish nuts with a soft texture. The shelled nuts may be stir-fried until green after which the outer skin will peel off easily. The peeled nuts are used for garnish on many special Korean dishes.

Ginseng (insam) is a much-prized root cultivated in Korea and China. This perennial herb is used mostly for medicinal purposes and is widely acclaimed for its rejuvenating qualities. It is usually sold dried, but fresh roots and rootlets are used in cooking. Ginseng tea and wine are popular in Korea.

Glutinous Rice (ch'apssal) is a white rice with a sticky consistency when cooked.

Glutinous Rice Flour (ch'apssal karu) is the flour from glutinous rice which is used in making Korean rice cakes.

Grain Syrup(choch'ŏng) is similar to dark corn syrup and is used as a sweetener. It is made by boiling "yot," a Korean candy base, with water and sugar until thick. Honey or sugar syrup can be used instead of this grain syrup in most recipes.

Green Onions: There are many varieties of green onions in Korea.
— (ch'ŏngp'a)—a medium sized variety harvested in the spring
— (puch'u)—a small, wild leek with a pungent flavor
— (shilp'a)—a thread-like onion with a taste similar to but stronger than chives
— (tallae)—a small, wild onion from the mountain meadows

Green Peppers, Korean (p'utkoch'u), are long, narrow unripe chili peppers and are usually hot to taste.

Indian Mustard Leaf (kat) is a green leaf available spring and autumn; Japanese "haruna."

Jujubes (taech'u) are similar to a date, usually used dried, for cooking or medicinal purposes. They should be soaked before using.

Kimchi is a spicy, slightly fermented pickle like vegetable dish accompanying every Korean meal. It is made from Chinese cabbage, Korean white radish, cucumber or other seasonal vegetables which are wilted with salt, stuffed with seasoning such as red pepper powder, chopped garlic, ginger juice and soused salted shrimp juice and fermented in earthenware crocks.

Konyak is jellied potato puree; it is sliced and used somewhat like a noodle.

Laver (kim) is cultivated carefully in the seabeds offshore in Korea and is of excellent quality. It is sold in packages of folded paper-thin sheets. It is used for wrapping rice rolls or broiled to a delicate crispness and served with a rice meal.

Lotus Root (yŏn-gūn) is the root of the lotus flower. It is grey on the outside but when cut open a beautiful lacy effect is formed in each slice by several open tubes which run the length of the root. It is served as a vegetable or candied as a sweet.

Malt Powder (yŏtkirūm) is dried sprouted barley which has been crushed into a powder. It is used to aid fermentation in making wines and drinks; it is a good food for yeast.

Mushrooms: There are several varieties used both fresh and dried.
— Brown oak mushrooms (p'yogo) (Japanese shiitake) are used in meat dishes after soaking well in warm water.
— Stone mushrooms (sōgi) also should be soaked before using.
— Jew's ear mushrooms (mogi) are large, delicate ear-shaped fungi.
— Pine mushrooms (songi) grow on pine tree trunks; they are most often sold fresh or canned; very tasty when sliced and sauteed.

Pear, Korean (pae) is a crisp, large, round, firm, sweet, apple-like pear which is very juicy. It has a tan outside skin and a cream-colored flesh with dark brown seeds. Harvested in the fall it keeps well in rice-hulls in a cool place. It is considered to be an aid in digestion.

Pine Nut (chat) is the nut-like edible, soft-textured, somewhat oily seeds of the pinon tree. They are used to make a gruel-soup and in garnishing drinks and other foods.

Pine Nut Powder is ground or finely chopped pine nuts used for rolling sweet rice cakes and other delicacies.

Pulgogi is Korea's best-known charcoal-broiled marinated beef dish. It is traditionally broiled over charcoal in a slotted pan but it may be oven-broiled or quickly pan-broiled.

Radish, Korean White (muu) is a round, long, firm white root much larger than a red or white table radish. The taste is sweet when first harvested and its texture is crisp and juicy. It is a basic kimchi ingredient; it is sometimes dried for making soups in the winter and small, young radishes are used for a special spring kimchi.

Red Pepper Paste (koch'ujang) is a dark reddish paste made from fermented soybean and red pepper powder mixed with glutinous rice flour and malt. It is spicy hot and widely used to thicken and season soups and stews. It will keep well in the refrigerator.

Red Peppers (koch'u) are a basic Korean seasoning ingredient. They are small, long peppers similar to cayenne and are hot to the taste. They are dried and ground or cut into threads or used fresh for seasoning or garnish. They are very high in vitamin A.

Rice Cake (ttŏk) is a delicacy served at most celebrations in Korea. It is made by steaming a glutinous rice flour dough which has been filled or mixed with various foods such as sesame seed, beans, mugwort, nuts, jujube, raisins; the dough is usually shaped beautifully into half-moons, circles or other soft shapes.

Rice Wine (ch'ŏngju) is a clear white wine made from rice used for drinking and cooking.

Salted Soused Shrimp (saeujŏt) are tiny shrimp which have been salted and become somewhat pickled and juicy; used in making kimchi and in seasoning.

Sesame Leaves (kkaennip) are the beautifully shaped pungent leaves of the sesame plant which are served as a vegetable in a sauce or deep-batter-fried.

Sesame Oil (ch'amgirūm) is pressed from toasted sesame seeds. It has a unique flavor and only a little is needed to add an authentic taste to Korean dishes.

Sesame Salt (kkaesogūm) is a mixture of toasted, crushed sesame seeds and salt. Add 1 teaspoon of salt to each cup of seeds. It is a basic Korean seasoning.

Sesame Seeds: White (hŭinkkae), black (kŏmŭnkkae) and round brown (tŭlkkae) are all used in Korean seasoning and in Korean candy-cookies.

Shinsollo is the name of a one-dish meal which is cooked at the table in a brass brazier "hot pot" which holds the charcoal in the center allowing the food to cook around it in a well-seasoned broth. It is a special occasion dish requiring hours of preserving preparation so that each food is cut precisely to the right shape and partially pre-cooked to allow for just the right last minute cooking at the table.

Soybean Paste (toenjang) is a thick brown paste made from a mixture of mashed fermented soybean lumps (left from making the soy sauce), powdered red pepper seeds and salt. It is used as a thickener for soups and stews and will keep well in the refrigerator.

Soy Sauce (kanjang) is a brownish-black salty liquid made by cooking fermented soybean cakes with water and salt. Each household in Korea used to make their own soy sauce in the spring; some still do. These are mild and add good flavor to most any food. Soy sauce is used in cooking, especially meats, but is also placed on the table to use as a dip for sauteed vegetables, fish and meat. The Japanese soy sauce is less salty but sweeter than Korean soy sauce.

Sweet Red Beans (p'at) are small and round and used widely in Korean confections. When cooked and mashed they are sweet and soft-textured. This sweet bean puree is used as filling in rice cakes and also now in donuts and rolls.

Todok is a fibrous white root found in the mountain in the spring. It must be pounded with a mallet and washed with salty water to take away its puckery taste before seasoning and cooking. It is an appetite stimulant.

Watercress (minari) is an aromatic plant used frequently in Korean cooking, especially the stems. It is not exactly the same as watercress but almost. The delicate leaves may be added to soups and are good with fish.

Most, if not all, of these ingredients may be purchased in Oriental groceries.

INDEX

INDEX OF KOREAN RECIPE TITLES